THE LITTLE BOOK OF ONENESS AND GOODNESS

Experiential Guidance from the World's Wisdom Traditions

Gudjon Bergmann

TABLE OF CONTENTS

GRATITUDE

This little book of quotes was made possible by those who have sought and experienced oneness and goodness throughout the ages.

To them, I am eternally grateful.

INTRODUCTION

Over the centuries, the world's religions have been enriched with a breadth and width of culture, history, dogma, and traditions. Trying to diminish their teachings to a few simple slogans is reductionism of the worst kind.

However… there are important overlaps. For instance, when teachings revolve around human experiences, such as our aspirations to do good and be good, our longing for peace of mind, and our wish to intentionally merge with the very nature of the universe, the traditions—especially the esoteric branches—offer insights and guidance that compliment each other.

This little book of quotes borrows wisdom from many traditions in an effort to

underline some of the more striking syn-
chronicities. The focus is on the experi-
ential aspects of spiritual practice, especially the two universal branches of oneness and goodness. The book includes
quotes from scriptures, scholars, religious
leaders, and wisdom seekers with the aim
of inspiring action and encouraging contemplation.

I have been gathering these quotes for
years (some have been with me for
decades) and many of them have become
an integral part of my spiritual practice.
It is my hope that they can serve as inspi-
ration for you as well and instigate fur-
ther research.

Blessings and peace,

Gudjon Bergmann
Interfaith Minister and Author
www.gudjonbergmann.com

Editorial note: I was raised a cultural
Christian and developed an intense in-
terest in Eastern mysticism in my early
twenties. Although I attempted to choose
quotes from a wide variety of sources for
this book, my personal interests are re-

flected in the selection. If you would like to add quotes from other traditions, please send them to me. I may include them in a later edition or share them on my social media channels.

GOODNESS

The world's wisdom traditions have provided humans with a variety of moral codes to live by, such as personal aspirations for goodness, guidelines for social cohesion, and restrictions on less desirable behaviors, including violence, greed, sensual gratification, and destructive emotions.

The general consensus has been synonymous. In addition to the inherent seeds of goodness within each and every human being—which need to be nurtured to fruition—a multitude of weeds exist that should be rooted out on a regular basis.

Restrictions can be thought of as discipline in a classroom. A modicum of discipline is needed for the optimum classroom environment, but practicing discipline for the sake of discipline will squeeze the life out of any environment. The same can be said of behavioral restrictions.

Practiced with understanding, they can create the perfect atmosphere for spiritual maturation. As a goal unto themselves, however, they create the spirituality of abstention and can often devolve into a religion of vigilance, where the behavior of others becomes more important to correct than ones own behavior.

Aspirations, on the other hand, give us something to strive for. The goal of anyone who aspires for goodness is to attain the very best of human qualities, including compassion, love, forgiveness, and empathy. Only a few ever reach the pinnacle of this quest, but the journey is never wasted. Minor improvements can reap major rewards.

The quotes in this section speak to all aspects of goodness—from restrictions to aspirations—starting with the most important topic.

LOVE

Spread love everywhere you go: first of all in your own house. Give love to your children, to your wife or husband, to a next-door neighbor. Let no one ever come to you without leaving better and happier. Be the living expression of God's kindness; kindness in your face, kindness in your eyes, kindness in your smile, kindness in your warm greeting.

Mother Teresa (1910-1997)
Albanian-Indian Roman Catholic Nun

For hatred can never put an end to hatred; love alone can. This is an unalterable law.

Verse 5, The Dhammapada
Collection of Sayings of the Buddha
Translated by Eknath Easwaran (1910-1999)

Do not be content with showing friendship in words alone, let your heart burn with loving kindness for all who may cross your path.

Baha'u'llah (1817-1892)
Founder of the Baha'i Faith

Thou shalt love the Lord thy God with all thy heart, and with all thy soul, and with all thy mind. This is the first and great commandment. And the second is like unto it, Thou shalt love thy neighbor as thyself. On these two commandments hang all the law and prophets.

St. Matthew 22:37-40
King James Bible

Freedom and love go together. Love is not a reaction. If I love you because you love me, that is mere trade, a thing to be bought in the market; it is not love. To love is not to ask anything in return, not even to feel that you are giving something- and it is only such love that can know freedom.

Jiddu Krishnamurti (1895-1986)
Indian Philosopher

True, this world of ours is full of hatred and disbelief, but that is no reason why we should not love and why we should not believe. We must love and believe in order to empty the hatred-sea.

Sri Chinmoy (1931-2007)
Indian Spiritual Leader

He that dwelleth in love, dwelleth in God. God is love. Therefore love. Without distinction, without calculation, without procrastination, love. Lavish it upon the poor, where it is very easy; especially upon the rich, who often need it most; most of all upon our equals, where it is very difficult, and for whom perhaps we do the least of all.

Henry Drummond (1851-1897)
Scottish Evangelist, Biologist and Writer

The medicine this sick world needs is love. Hatred must be replaced by love, and fear by faith that love will prevail.

Peace Pilgrim
Mildred L. Norman (1908-1981)
Non-denominational Spiritual Teacher

Lord, make me an instrument of thy peace. Where there is hatred, let me sow love; where there is injury, pardon; where there is doubt, faith; where there is despair, hope; where there is darkness, light; and where there is sadness, joy.

St. Francis of Assisi (1182-1226)
Italian Roman Catholic Friar and Preacher

All love is expansion, all selfishness is contraction. Love is therefore the only law of life. He who loves lives, he who is selfish is dying. Therefore love for love's sake, because it is law of life, just as you breathe to live.

Swami Vivekananda (1863-1902)
Hindu Monk and Disciple of Ramakrishna

Love seeks one thing only; the good of the one loved. It leaves all the other secondary effects to take care of themselves. Love, therefore, is its own reward.

Father Thomas Merton (1915-1968)
American Catholic Writer, Monk, and Mystic

Ordinary love is selfish, darkly rooted in desires and satisfactions. Divine love is without condition, without boundary, without change. The flux of the human heart is gone forever at the transfixing touch of pure love.

Swami Sri Yukteswar Giri (1855-1936)
Indian Guru and Teacher to Yogananda

And like the fish, swimming in the vast sea and resting in its deeps, and like the bird, boldly mounting high in the sky, so the soul feels its spirit freely moving through the vastness and the depth and the unutterable richness of love.

Beatrice of Nazareth (1200-1268)
Flemish Cistercian Nun

The truth is, indeed, that love is the threshold of another universe. Beyond the vibrations with which we are familiar, the rainbow-like range of its colours is still in full growth. But, for all the fascination that the lower shades have for us, it is only towards the "ultra" that the creation of light advances. It is in these invisible and, we might almost say, immaterial zones that we can look for true initiation into unity. The depths we attribute to matter are no more than the reflection of the peaks of spirit.

Pierre Teilhard de Chardin (1881-1955)
Jesuit Catholic Priest and Philosopher

WHAT TO AVOID?

Hold back your mind from pride, for pride comes only from ignorance. The man who does not know thinks that he is great, that he has done this or that great thing; the wise man knows that only God is great, that all good work is done by God alone.

Jiddu Krishnamurti (1895-1986)
Indian Philosopher

Beware of lust; it corrupteth both the body and the mind.

Zoroaster (ca. 1000 BCE)
Iranian prophet and founder of Zoroastrianism

There is no fire like lust, no sickness like hatred, no sorrow like separateness, no joy like peace. No disease is worse than greed, no suffering worse than selfish passion. Know this, and seek nirvana as the highest joy.

Verses 202-203, The Dhammapada
Collection of Sayings of the Buddha
Translated by Eknath Easwaran (1910-1999)

If you have a particular bad habit or karmic inclination, don't mix with those who have the same kind of bad habit. If you tend to be greedy, avoid the company of others who are greedy. If you have a desire to drink, stay away from those who drink. People who support your bad habits are not your friends. They will cause you to throw away your soul's joy. Avoid the company of wrongdoers and mix with those who are good.

Paramahansa Yogananda (1893-1952)
Founder of the Self-Realization Fellowship

Thou shalt have no other gods before me. Honor thy father and thy mother. Remember the sabbath day, to keep it holy. Thou shalt not make unto thee any graven image. Thou shalt not take the name of the Lord thy God in vain. Thou shalt not kill. Thou shalt not commit adultery. Thou shalt not steal. Thou shalt not bear false witness against thy neighbor. Thou shalt not covet.

The Hebrew Bible

Materialism, attachment to things of the world, includes pride. Many religious people suffer from pride: taking pleasure or even delight in being good, or religious.

Idries Shah (1924-1996)
Author and Teacher of the Sufi tradition

I have been all things unholy. If God can work through me, he can work through anyone.

St. Francis of Assisi (1182-1226)
Roman Catholic Friar and Preacher

Sickness, mental laziness, doubt, lack of enthusiasm, sloth, craving for sense-pleasure, false perception, despair caused by failure to concentrate and unsteadiness in concentration; these distractions are the obstacles to knowledge.

How to Know God: The Yoga Aphorisms of Patanjali,
translated by Prabhavananda (1893-1976) and Isher-
wood (1904-1986)

Jealousies, hatreds, and revenge can lead to violence that, unless checked, rips communities to pieces. Murder instigates blood feuds that drag on indefinitely. Sex, if it violates certain restraints, can rouse passions so intense as to destroy entire communities. Similarly with theft and prevarication. We can imagine societies in which people do exactly as they please on these counts, but none have been found and anthropologists have now covered the globe. Apparently, if total permissiveness has ever been tried, its inventors have not survived for anthropologists to study.

Huston Smith (1919-2016)
American Religious Studies Scholar

The mind may be said to be of two kinds, pure and impure. Driven by the senses it becomes impure; but with the senses under control, the mind becomes pure. It is the mind that frees or enslaves. Driven by the senses we become bound; master of the senses we become free. Those who seek freedom must master their senses.

Amritabindu Upanishad
Translated by Eknath Easwaran (1910-1999)

The very purpose of religion is to control yourself, not to criticize others. Rather, we must criticize ourselves. How much am I doing about my anger? About my attachment, about my hatred, about my pride, my jealousy? These are the things which we must check in daily life.

The 14th Dalai Lama
Gelug School of Tibetan Buddhism

Lose your temper and you lose a friend;
lie and you lose yourself.

Hopi Proverb

Thinking about sense-objects will attach
you to sense-objects; Grow attached and
you become addicted; Thwart your ad-
diction, it turns to anger; Be angry, and
you confuse your mind; Confuse your
mind, your forget the lesson of experience; Forget experience, you lose discrimination; Lose discrimination, and you
miss life's only purpose.

The Bhagavad Gita
Translated by Prabhavananda (1893-1976)
and Isherwood (1904-1986)

ASPIRATIONS

Speak the truth. Do your duty. Neglect
not the scriptures. Give your best to your
teacher. Do not cut off the line of prog-
eny. Swerve not from the truth. Swerve
not from the good. Protect your spiritual
progress always. Give your best in learn-
ing and teaching. Never fail to respect the
sages. See the divine in your mother, fa-

ther, teacher and guest. Never do what is wrong. Honor those who are worthy of honor. Give with faith. Give with love. Give with joy. If you are in doubt about right conduct, follow the example of the sages, who know what is best for spiritual growth. This is the instruction of the Vedas; this is the secret; this is the message.

Taittiriya Upanishad
Translated by Eknath Easwaran (1910-1999)

Goodness needeth not to enter into the soul, for it is already there, only it is unperceived.

Theologia Germanica

Seek to make your life long and its purpose in the service of your people. Prepare a noble death song for the day when you go over the great divide. Always give a word or a sign of salute when meeting or passing a friend, even a stranger, when in a lonely place. Show respect to all people and grovel to none.

Chief Tecumseh (1768-1813)
Shawnee Nation

Blessed are the poor in spirit: for theirs is the kingdom of heaven. Blessed are they that mourn: for they shall be comforted. Blessed are the meek: for they shall inherit the earth. Blessed are they which do hunger and thirst after righteousness: for they shall be filled. Blessed are the merciful: for they shall obtain mercy. Blessed are the pure in heart: for they shall see God. Blessed are the peacemakers: for they shall be called the children of God.

St. Matthew 5:3-9
King James Bible

Ye have heard that it hath been said, an eye for an eye, and a tooth for a tooth, but I say unto you, that ye resist not evil but whosoever shall smite thee on thy right cheek, turn to him the other also.

St. Matthew 5:38-39
King James Bible

Keep a clear eye towards life's end. Do not forget your purpose and destiny as God's creature. What you are in his sight is what you are and nothing more. Remember that when you leave this earth, you can take nothing that you have received... but only what you have given; a full heart enriched by honest service, love, sacrifice, and courage.

St. Francis of Assisi (1182-1226)
Italian Roman Catholic Friar and Preacher

The demands of Jesus are difficult because they require us to do something extraordinary. At the same time He asks us to regard these [acts of goodness] as something usual, ordinary.

Albert Schweitzer (1875-1965)
French-German Theologian and Physician

Undisturbed calmness of the mind is attained by cultivating friendliness toward the happy, compassion for the unhappy, delight in the virtuous, and indifference toward the wicked.

How to Know God: The Yoga Aphorisms of Patanjali,
translated by Prabhavananda (1893-1976) and Isher-
wood (1904-1986)

There's a light seed grain inside
You fill it with yourself or it dies

Rumi (1207-1273)
Persian Poet, Islamic Scholar and Sufi Mystic

Whatever is noble, whatever is right, whatever is pure, whatever is lovely, whatever is admirable—if anything is excellent or praiseworthy—think about such things.

Philippians 4:8
The Bible

When something painful or disagreeable happens to me, instead of a melancholy look, I answer by a smile. At first I did not always succeed, but now it has become a habit which I am glad to have acquired.

Saint Thérèse de Lisieux (1873-1897)
Roman Catholic French Carmelite Nun

The best thing to give your enemy is forgiveness; to an opponent, tolerance; to a friend, your heart; to your child, a good example; to your father, deference; to your mother, conduct that will make her proud of you; to your self, respect; to all men charity.

Swami Sivananda Saraswati (1887-1963)
Hindu Spiritual Teacher and Proponent of Yoga

The highest education is that which does not merely give us information but makes our life in harmony with all existence.

Rabindranath Tagore (1861-1941)
Bengali Poet and Writer

If there is to be peace in the world, there must be peace in the nations.
If there is to be peace in the nations, there must be peace in the cities.
If there is to be peace in the cities,
there must be peace between neighbors.
If there is to be peace between neighbors, there must be peace in the home.
If there is to be peace in the home, there must be peace in the heart.

Lao Tzu (6th Century BC)
Legendary Chinese Figure (Taoism)

RECIPROCATION (GOLDEN RULE)

Therefore all things whatsoever ye would that men should do to you, do ye even so to them: for this is the law and the prophets.

St. Matthew 7:12
King James Bible

If one is cruel to himself, how can we expect him to be compassionate with others?

Hasdai ibn Shaprut (915-970)
Jewish Scholar and Patron of Science

Do not impose on others what you yourself do not desire.

Confucius (551-479 BC)
Chinese Philosopher (Confucianism)

I am a lover, and I deal in love. Sow flowers, so your surroundings become a garden. Don't sow thorns; for they will prick your feet. We are all one body. Whoever tortures another, wounds himself.

Rahman Baba (1653-1711)
Pashtun Sufi Dervish and Poet from Peshawar

None of you truly believes until he wishes for his brother what he wishes for himself.

40 Hadith (number 13)
Imam al-Nawawi (1233-1277)

What is hateful to you, do not do to your fellow: this is the whole Torah; the rest is the explanation; go and learn.

Shabbath folio:31a, Babylonian Talmud

Treat those who are good with goodness, and also treat those who are not good with goodness. Thus goodness is attained. Be honest to those who are honest, and also be honest to those who are not honest. Thus honesty is attained.

Lao Tzu (6th Century BC)
Legendary Chinese Figure (Taoism)

SERVICE

Kindness in word creates confidence. Kindness in thinking creates profoundness. Kindness in giving creates love.

Lao Tzu (6th Century BCE)
Legendary Chinese Figure (Taoism)

Help your brothers boat across, and your own will reach the shore.

Hindu proverb

Do all the good you can. By all the means you can. In all the ways you can. In all the places you can. At all the times you can. To all the people you can. As long as ever you can.

John Wesley (1703-1791)
Anglican Cleric and Founder of Methodism

Then shall the righteous answer him, saying, Lord, when saw we thee hunger, and fed thee? Or thirst, and gave thee drink? When saw we thee a stranger, and took thee in? Or naked, and clothed thee? Or when saw we thee sick, or in prison, and came unto thee? And the King shall answer and say unto them, Verily I say unto you, Inasmuch as ye have done it unto one of the least of these brethren, ye have done it unto me.

St. Matthew 25:40
King James Bible

Find out how much God has given you and from it take what you need; the remainder is needed by others.

Saint Augustine (354-430)
Early Christian theologian

I slept and dreamt that life was joy. I awoke and saw that life was service. I acted and behold, service was joy.

Rabindranath Tagore (1861-1941)
Bengali Poet and Writer

Doing good to others is not a duty. It is a joy, for it increases your own health and happiness.

Zoroaster (ca. 1000 BCE)
Iranian prophet and founder of Zoroastrianism

Our prime purpose in this life is to help others. And if you can't help them, at least don't hurt them.

The 14th Dalai Lama (1935)
Gelug School of Tibetan Buddhism

The best way to find yourself is to lose yourself in the service of others.

Mahatma Gandhi (1869-1948)
Civil Rights Leader and Nonviolent Visionary

FORGIVENESS & NONVIOLENCE

Nonviolence is the answer to the crucial political and moral question of our time —the need for mankind to overcome oppression and violence without resorting to violence and oppression... Sooner or later all the people of the world will have to discover a way to live together in peace and thereby transform this pending cosmic elegy into a creative psalm of brotherhood. If this is to be achieved mankind must evolve for all human conflict, a method that rejects revenge, aggression, and retaliation. The foundation of such a method is love.

Martin Luther King Jr. (1929-1968)
Baptist Minister and Civil Rights Leader

Father, forgive them; for they know not what they do.

St. Luke 23:34
King James Bible

An eye for an eye will only make the whole world blind.

Mahatma Gandhi (1869-1948)
Civil Rights Leader and Nonviolent Visionary

To be wronged is nothing unless you continue to remember it.

Confucius (551-479 BCE)
Philosopher (Confucianism)

The cure for hatred is straightforward. One should pray for the person toward whom he feels hatred; make specific supplication mentioning this person by name, asking God to give this person good things in this life and the next. When one does this with sincerity, hearts mend. If one truly wants to purify his or her heart and root out disease, there must be total sincerity and conviction that these cures are effective.

Hamza Yusuf (1958)
American Islamic Scholar and Author

And when you stand praying, if you hold anything against anyone, forgive them, so that your Father in heaven may forgive you your sins.

Mark 11:25
King James Bible

The best revenge is to be unlike him who performed the injury.

Marcus Aurelius (121-180)
Roman Emperor

FAITH AND BELIEF

It is impossible to present a religiously oriented quote book without addressing God, beliefs, and personal faith. The following quotes touch on those three topics and come at them from a variety perspectives.

God is the great unknown, the ultimate mystery. Spiritual maturity asks that we set aside certainty and learn to hold opposing thoughts in our minds for contemplation, rather than taking the easy route of accepting or rejecting ideas without investigation.

Keep an open mind as you read the following.

WHERE IS GOD?

O Lord, forgive three sins that are due to my human limitations. Thou art everywhere, but I worship you here; thou art without form, but I worship you in these forms; thou needest no praise, yet I offer you these prayers and salutations. Lord, forgive three sins that are due to my human limitations.

Hindu Invocation
Used at Opening Ceremonies at Temples

Christian terminology employs two phrases—God immanent and God transcendent—which make a similar distinction. Again and again, in Hindu and Christian literature, we find this great paradox restated—that God is both within and without, instantly present and infinitely elsewhere, the dweller in the atom and the abode of all things. But this is the same Reality, the same Godhead, seen in its two relations to the cosmos (...) They imply no kind of duality. Atman and Brahman are one.

Swami Prabhavananda (1893-1976)
and Christopher Isherwood (1904-1986)

God writes the Gospel not in the Bible alone, but also on trees, and in the flowers and clouds and stars.

Martin Luther (1483-1546)
German Professor of Theology (Lutheranism)

Those who cherish God in the sun witness the sun, and those who cherish Him in living things observe a living thing, and those who cherish Him in lifeless things view a lifeless thing, and those who cherish Him as a unique and unequalled being see Him as such. Beware of committing yourself exclusively to a specific belief so that you disbelieve everything else, or else you will miss out on much good—in fact, you will miss out on recognizing the authentic truth. God, the all-present and all-powerful, is not limited to any single belief.

Ibn al-Arabi (1165-1240)
Scholar of Islam and Sufi Mystic

Deep down in every man, woman and child, is the fundamental idea of God. It may be obscured by calamity, by pomp, by worship of other things, but in some form or another it is there. For faith in a

Power greater than ourselves, and miraculous demonstrations of that power in human lives, are facts as old as man himself.

Alcoholic Anonymous
Big Book of AA

Thou must love God as not-God, not-Spirit, not-person, not-image, but as He is, a sheer, pure absolute One, sundered from all two-ness, and in whom we must eternally sink from nothingness to nothingness.

Meister Eckhart (1260-1328)
German Theologian, Philosopher, and Mystic

Whatever you think concerning God—know that he is different from that!

Ibn Ata Allah (1259-1310)
Third Murshid of the Shadhili Sufi Order

There is but One God, His name is Truth, He is the Creator, He fears none, he is without hate, He never dies, He is beyond the cycle of births and death, He is self illuminated, He is realized by the kindness of the True Guru. He was True in the beginning, He was True when the ages commenced and has ever been True, He is also True now.

Guru Nanak (1469-1539)
Founder of Sikhism

No statement about God is simply, literally true. God is far more than can be measured, described, defined in ordinary language, or pinned down to any particular thing.

David Jenkins (1925-2016)
Theologian and Bishop of Durham in England

Are you looking for me? I am in the next seat. My shoulder is against yours. You will not find me in the stupas, not in Indian shrine rooms, nor in synagogues, nor in cathedrals:
not in masses, nor kirtans, not in legs winding around your own neck, nor in eating nothing but vegetables. When you really look for me, you will see me instantly—you will find me in the tiniest house of time.

Kabir (1440-1518)
Poet, Indian Mystic and Saint

The principle of any science is invisible, theoretical, as is our idea of Spirit. No one has seen God; no one has seen Life; what we have seen is the manifestation of Life. No one has seen Intelligence; we experience it. No one has ever seen Causation; we can see what It does, we deal with Its effects. We do not see Beauty. The artist feels beauty and depicts it as best he can, and the result of his effort is what we call the beautiful...We do not see Life, we experience living. Causation is invisible.

Ernest Holmes (1887-1960)
Founder of Religious Science

Wherever you look...see that one unique Presence, indivisible and eternal, is manifested in all the universe. That is because God impregnates all things.

Anandamayi Ma (1896-1982)
Bengali Saint

God is the experience of looking at a tree and saying, 'Ah!

Joseph Campbell (1904-1987)
American Mythologist, Writer and Lecturer

When somebody says to me, "I don't believe in God," my first response is, "Tell me about the God you don't believe in." Almost always, it's the God of supernatural theism.

Marcus J. Borg (1942-2015)
New Testament Scholar, Theologian and Author

You see many stars in the sky at night, but not when the sun rises. Can you therefore say that there are no stars in the heavens during the day? Because you cannot find God in the days of your ignorance, say not that there is no God.

Ramakrishna (1836-1886)
Indian Yogi and Mystic

God is like a mirror. The mirror never changes, but everybody who looks at it sees something different.

Rabbi Harold Kushner (1935)
Prominent American Rabbi and Popular Author

Every content of the universe is throbbing with the Life of the Lord. Smile with the flowers and the green grass. Smile with the shrubs, ferns and twigs. Develop friendship with all neighbors, dogs, cats, cows, human beings, trees, in fact, with all nature's creations. You will have a perfect and rich life.

Swami Sivananda Saraswati (1887-1963)
Hindu Spiritual Teacher and Proponent of Yoga

ONE SUN, MANY RAYS

Like the bee gathering honey from different flowers, the wise man accepts the essence of different Scriptures and sees only good in all religions.

Srimad Bhagavatam

God has made different religions to suit different aspirants, times, and countries. All doctrines are only so many paths; but a path is by no means God himself. Indeed, one can reach God if one follows any of the paths with whole-hearted devotion. One may eat a cake with icing either straight or sidewise. It will taste sweet either way.

Ramakrishna (1836-1886)
Indian Yogi and Mystic

Do not be idolatrous about or bound to any doctrine, theory, or ideology, even Buddhist ones. All systems of thought are guiding means; they are not absolute truth.

Thich Nhat Hanh (1926)
Vietnamese Buddhist Monk and Peace Activist

God is not a Christian, God is not a Jew, or a Muslim, or a Hindu, or a Buddhist. All of those are human systems, which human beings have created to try to help us walk into the mystery of God. I honor my tradition, I walk through my tradition, but I don't think my tradition defines God, I think it only points me to God.

John Shelby Spong (1931)
American Bishop of the Episcopal Church

Now there are diversities of gifts, but the same Spirit. And there are differences of administrations, but the same Lord.

Corinthians 12:4-5
King James Bible

It is, then, by those shadows of the hoary Past and their fantastic silhouettes on the external screen of every religion and philosophy, that we can, by checking them as we go along, and comparing them, trace out finally the body that produced them.

Helena Blavatsky (1831-1891)
Co-Founder of the Theosophical Society

O Marvel! A garden amidst the flames. My heart has become capable of every form: It is a pasture for gazelles and a convent for Christian monks, and a temple for idols and the pilgrim's Kaa'ba, and the tables of the Torah and the book of the Qur'an. I follow the religion of Love: whatever way Love's camels take. That is my religion and my faith.

Ibn al-Arabi (1165-1240)
Scholar of Islam and Sufi Mystic

It is the duty of every cultured man or woman to read sympathetically the scriptures of the world. If we are to respect others' religions, as we would have them respect our own, a friendly study of the world's religions is a sacred duty.

Mahatma Gandhi (1869-1948)
Civil Rights Leader and Nonviolent Visionary

The varieties of religious belief are an advantage, since all faiths are good, so far as they encourage us to lead a religious life. The more sects there are, the more opportunities there are for making a successful appeal to the divine instinct in all of us.

Swami Vivekananda (1863-1902)
Hindu Monk and Disciple of Ramakrishna

Indian religion has always felt that since the minds, the temperaments and the intellectual affinities of men are unlimited in their variety, a perfect liberty of thought and of worship must be allowed to the individual in his approach to the Infinite.

Sri Aurobindo (1872-1950)
Hindu Philosopher, Yogi, Guru and Poet

I love you when you bow in your mosque, kneel in your temple, pray in your church. For you and I are sons of one religion, and it is the spirit.

Khalil Gibran (1883-1931)
Lebanese-American Artist, Poet and Writer

Theologians may quarrel, but the mystics of the world speak the same language.

Meister Eckhart (1260-1328)
German Theologian, Philosopher and Mystic

BEING A BELIEVER

The Christian shoemaker does his duty not by putting little crosses on the shoes, but by making good shoes, because God is interested in good craftsmanship.

Martin Luther (1483-1546)
German Professor of Theology (Lutheranism)

It is easy enough to be friendly to one's friends. But to befriend the one who regards himself as your enemy is the quintessence of true religion. The other is mere business.

Mahatma Gandhi (1869-1948)
Civil Rights Leader and Nonviolent Visionary

There is no compulsion in religion

The Qur'an 2:256

A religious man is a person who holds God and man in one thought at one time, at all times, who suffers harm done to others, whose greatest compassion, whose greatest strength is love and defiance of despair.

Abraham Joshua Heschel (1907-1972)
Polish-born American Rabbi

The Sufi recognizes the knowledge of self as the essence of all religions; he traces it in every religion, he sees the same truth in each, and therefore he regards all as one. Hence he can realize the saying of Jesus; 'I and my Father are one.' The difference between creature and Creator remains on his lips, not in his soul.

Hazrat Inayat Khan (1882-1927)
Teacher of Universal Sufism

PRAYER

Morning and evening I seek You, spreading out my hands, lifting up my face in prayer. I sigh for You with a thirsting heart; I am like the pauper begging at my doorstep. The heights of heaven cannot contain Your presence, yet You have a dwelling in my mind. I try to conceal Your glorious name in my heart, but my desire for You grows till it bursts out of my mouth. Therefore I shall praise the name of the Lord as long as the breath of the living God is in my nostrils.

Solomon ibn Gabriol (1021-1058)
Andalusian Poet and Jewish Philosopher

And when thou prayest, thou shalt not be as the hypocrites are: for they love to pray standing in the synagogues and in the corners of the streets, that they may be seen of men. Verily I say unto you, they have their reward. But thou, when though hast shut thy door, pray to thy Father which is in secret; and thy Father which seeth in secret shall reward thee openly.

St. Matthew 6:6
King James Bible

For prayer is nothing else than being on terms of friendship with God.

Saint Teresa of Avila (1515-1582)
Carmelite Nun and Catholic Saint

Our prayers should be for blessings in general, for God knows best what is good for us.

Socrates (470-399 BC)
Greek Philosopher

I have held many things in my hands, and I have lost them all; but whatever I have placed in God's hands, that I still possess.

Martin Luther (1483-1546)
German Professor of Theology (Lutheranism)

When I admire the wonders of a sunset or the beauty of the moon, my soul expands in the worship of the creator.

Mahatma Gandhi (1869-1948)
Civil Rights Leader and Nonviolent Visionary

My God and my Lord: eyes are at rest, the stars are setting, hushed are the movements of birds in their nests, of monsters in the deep. And you are the Just who knows no change, the Equity that does not swerve, the Everlasting that never passes away. The doors of kings are locked and guarded by their henchmen, but your door is open to those who call upon you. My Lord, each lover is

now alone with his beloved. And I am
alone with you.

Rabia al Basri (713-801)
Female Muslim Saint and Sufi Mystic

I pray on the principle that wine knocks
the cork out of a bottle. There is an in-
ward fermentation, and there must be a
went.

Henry Ward Beecher (1813-1887)
Clergyman and Social Reformer

Our Lord told us to pray in secret—that
means in your heart—and he instructed
us to "shut the door." What is this door
he says we must shut, if not the mouth?
For we are the temple in which Christ
dwells, for as the Apostle said: "You are
the temple of the Lord." And the Lord
enters into your inner self into this house,
to cleanse it from everything that is un-
clean, but only while the door—that is,
your mouth—is closed shut.

Aphrahat the Persian (270-345)
Syriac-Christian Author

There are two main pitfalls on the road
to mastery of the art of prayer. If a per-

son gets what he asks for, his humility is in danger. If he fails to get what he asks for, he is apt to lose confidence. Indeed, no matter whether prayer seems to be succeeding or failing, humility and confidence are two virtues which are absolutely essential.

Anonymous Trappist Monk

Prayer does not change God, but it changes him who prays.

Soren Kierkegaard (1813-1855)
Danish Philosopher and Religious Author

SEEKING

I would like the church to be a place where the questions of people are honored rather than a place where we have all the answers. The church has to get out of propaganda. The future will involve us in more interfaith dialogue. We cannot say we have the only truth.

John Shelby Spong (1931)
American Bishop of the Episcopal Church

Therefore, Ananda, be ye lamps unto yourselves, be ye refuge to yourselves. Betake yourselves to no external refuge. Hold fast to the Truth as a lamp; hold fast to the Truth as a refuge. Look not for a refuge in anyone beside yourselves.

Mahaparinibbana Sutta

We cannot live in a world that is interpreted for us by others. An interpreted world is not a hope. Part of the terror is to take back our own listening. To use our own voice. To see our own light.

Hildegard of Bingen (1098-1179)
Benedictine Abbess and Christian Mystic

There are few contemplatives, because few souls are perfectly humble.

Thomas a Kempis (1380-1471)
German-Dutch Canon

Do not seek to follow in the footsteps of the men of old; seek what they sought.

Matsuo Basho (1644-1694)
Japanese Poet

Seek, and ye shall find.

Matthew 7:7
King James Bible

PRACTICE

Those who recite many scriptures but fail to practice their teachings are like a cowherd counting another's cows. They do not share in the joys of the spiritual life. But those who know few scriptures yet practice their teachings, overcoming all lust, hatred, and delusion, live with a pure mind in the highest wisdom. They stand without external supports and share in the joys of the spiritual life.

Verses 19-20
The Dhammapada
Collection of Sayings of the Buddha
Translated by Eknath Easwaran (1910-1999)

There is one inevitable criterion of judgment touching religious faith in doctrinal matters. Can you reduce it to practice? If not, have none of it.

Hosea Ballou (1771-1852)
American Universalist Clergyman

The distinctive aspect of mysticism is something that cannot be understood by study, but only by dhawq [tasting/immediate experience]. There is a big difference between knowing the meaning and causes of health and satiety, and being healthy and satisfied.

Al-Ghazali (1058-1111)
Persian Philosopher and Muslim Theologian

Who knows the flower best? - the one who reads about it in a book, or the one who finds it wild on the mountainside?

Alexandra David-Neel (1868-1969)
Belgian-French Explorer and Spiritualist

Those who are more adapted to the active life can prepare themselves for contemplation in the practice of the active life, while those who are more adapted to the contemplative life can take upon themselves the works of the active life as to become yet more apt for contemplation.

St. Thomas Aquinas (1225-1274)
Italian Dominican Friar and Philosopher

Spiritual practice is not just sitting and meditation. Practice is looking, thinking, touching, drinking, eating and talking. Every act, every breath, and every step can be practice and can help us to become more ourselves.

Thich Nhat Hanh (1926)
Vietnamese Monk and Peace Activist

Success in yoga comes quickly to those who are intensely energetic. Success varies according to the means adopted to attain it—mild, medium, or intense.

How to Know God: The Yoga Aphorisms of Patanjali,
translated by Prabhavananda (1893-1976) and Isher-
wood (1904-1986)

As a single footstep will not make a path on the earth, so a single thought will not make a pathway in the mind. To make a deep physical path, we walk again and again. To make a deep mental path, we must think over and over the kind of thoughts we wish to dominate our lives.

Henry David Thoreau (1817-1862)
Transcendentalist and Philosopher

Religion is doing; a man does not merely think his religion or feel it, he 'lives' his religion as much as he is able, otherwise it is not religion but fantasy or philosophy. Whether he likes it or not he shows his attitude towards religion by his actions and he can show his attitude only by his actions. Therefore if his actions are opposed to those which are demanded by a given religion he cannot assert that he belongs to that religion.

G.I. Gurdjieff (1866-1949)
Mystic, Philosopher and Spiritual Teacher

You must find out a way of living differently. That depends on you, and not on someone else, because in this there is no teacher, no pupil; there is no leader; there is no guru; there is no Master, no Savior. You yourself are the teacher and the pupil; you are the Master; you are the guru; you are the leader; you are everything.

Jiddu Krishnamurti (1895-1986)
Indian Philosopher

The truth indeed has never been preached by the Buddha, seeing that one has to realize it within oneself.

Sutralankara

ONENESS

The concept of oneness has mostly been prevalent in Eastern mysticism, and yet it has surfaced in some shape or form in most of the wisdom traditions.

Paradoxically, oneness is not a single concept. Across different traditions it has been referred to as *symbiosis* (earthly interdependence), *unity* (close relationship), *two sides of the same coin* (yin-yang), or, most commonly, *nonduality* (one without a second).

Whatever it has been called, select groups of human beings from all traditions have always sought to consciously merge with the infinite oneness from which they emerged, that part of the universe that is always present and never changes.

The following quotes speak to both the philosophy and practice of oneness.

THOU ART THAT

The soul is in God and God in the soul, just as the fish is in the sea and the sea in the fish.

Saint Catherine of Siena (1347-1380)
Scholastic Philosopher and Theologian

In the beginning was only being, one without a second. Out of himself he brought forth the cosmos and entered into everything in it. There is nothing that does not come from him. Of everything he is the inmost Self. He is the truth; he is the Self supreme. You are that, Shvetaketu; you are that.

Chandogya Upanishad
Translated by Eknath Easwaran (1910-1999)

When it's cold, water freezes into ice; when it's warm, ice melts into water.

Similarly, when you are confused, essence freezes into mind; when you are enlightened, mind melts into essence.

Muso Soseki (1275-1351)
Rinzai Zen Buddhist Monk and Poet

The first peace, which is the most important, is that which comes within the souls of people when they realize their relationship, their oneness, with the universe and all its powers; and when they realize that at the center of the universe dwells Wakan-Taka (the Great Spirit); and that this center is really everywhere, it is within each of us. This is the real peace, and the others are but reflections of this. The second peace is that which is made between two individuals; and the third is that which is made between two nations. But above all, you should understand that there can never be peace between nations until there is known that true peace, which, as I have often said, is within the souls of men.

Black Elk (1863-1950)
Medicine Man of the Oglala Lakota (Sioux)

The soul of all is one soul and the truth is one truth, under whatever religion it is hidden.

Hazrat Inayat Khan (1882-1927)
Teacher of Universal Sufism

Now there are diversities of gifts, but the same Spirit. And there are differences of administrations, but the same Lord.

Corinthians 12:4-5
King James Bible

Behind the light in every little bulb is a great dynamic current; beneath every little wave is the vast ocean, which has become the many waves. So it is with human beings. God made every man in His image [Genesis 1:27], and gave each one freedom. But you forget the Source of your being and the unequaled power of God that is an inherent part of you.

Paramahansa Yogananda (1893-1952)
Founder of the Self-Realization Fellowship

Before our body existed, one energy was already there. Like jade, more lustrous as it's polished; like gold, brighter as it's refined. Sweep clear the ocean of birth and

death. Stay firm by the door of total
mastery, a particle at the point of open
awareness. The gentle firing is warm.

Sun Bu'er (1119-1182)
Taoist Master

The eye through which I see God is the
same eye through which God sees me;
my eye and God's eye are one eye, one
seeing, one knowing, one love.

Meister Eckhart (1260-1328)
German Theologian, Philosopher and Mystic

From out of all the many particulars
comes oneness, and out of oneness come
all the many particulars.

Heraclitus (ca. 500 BC)
Greek Philosopher

The Beloved is all in all; the lover merely
veils Him; The Beloved is all that lives,
the lover a dead thing.

Rumi (1207-1273)
Persian Poet, Islamic Scholar and Sufi Mystic

What is nature to him? There is never a beginning, there is never an end, to the inexplicable continuity of this web of God, but always circular power returning into itself. Therein it resembles his own spirit, whose beginning, whose ending, he never can find,—so entire, so boundless.

Ralph Waldo Emerson (1803-1882)
American Essayist and Transcendentalist

Talk as much philosophy as you please, worship as many gods as you like, observe all ceremonies, sing devoted praises to any number of divine beings—liberation never comes, even at the end of a hundred aeons, without the realization of the Oneness of the Self.

Adi Shankara (788-820)
Indian Philosopher and Theologian

There is one breath. There is one life. There is one earth. All is holy. All is sacred. All is one.

Sisters of Earth in Holyoke, Massachusetts

This we know. The Earth does not belong to us; we belong to the Earth. All things are connected, like the blood that unites one family. Whatever befalls the Earth, befalls the children of the Earth. We do not weave the web of life; we are only a strand of it. Whatever we do to the web, we do to ourselves.

Chief Seattle, (1786-1866)
Native American Chief of the Suquamish Tribe

Learn to look with an equal eye upon all beings, seeing the one Self in all.

Srimad Bhagavatam

Troubled or still, water is always water. What difference can embodiment or dis-embodiment make to the Liberated? Whether calm or in tempest, the same-ness of the Ocean suffers no change.

Yogavasistha

OUR ESSENTIAL NATURE

A wife loves her husband not for his own sake, dear, but because the Self lives in him. A husband loves his wife not for her own sake, dear, but because the Self lives in her. Children are loved not for the own sake, but because the Self lives in them. Wealth is loved not for its own sake, but because the Self lives in it. Brahmins are loved not for their own sake, but because the Self lives in them. The universe is loved not for its own sake, but because the Self lives in it. The gods are love not for their own sake, but because the Self lives in them. Creatures are loved not for their own sake, but because the Self lives in them. Everything is loved not for its own sake, but because the Self lives in it. This Self has to be realized.

Brihadaranyaka Upanishad
Translated by Eknath Easwaran (1910-1999)

Know this Atman
Unborn, undying,
Never ceasing,
Never beginning,
Deathless, birthless,
Unchanging forever.

Bhagavad Gita
Translated by Prabhavananda (1893-1976)
and Isherwood (1904-1986)

I died a mineral, and became a plant. I died a plant and rose an animal. I died an animal and was a man. Why should I fear? When was I less by dying? Yet once more I shall die as man, to soar with the blessed angels; but even from angelhood I must pass on. All except God perishes. When I have sacrificed my angel soul, I shall become that which no mind ever conceived. O, let me not exist! for Non-Existence proclaims, To Him we shall return.

Rumi (1207-1273)
Persian Poet, Islamic Scholar and Sufi Mystic

That which makes the tongue speak but cannot be spoken by the tongue, know that as the Self. This Self is not someone other than you. That which makes the mind think but cannot be thought by the mind, that is the Self indeed. This Self is not someone other than you. That which makes the eye see but cannot be seen by the eye, that is the Self indeed. This Self is not someone other than you. That which makes the ear hear but cannot be heard by the ear, that is the Self indeed. This Self is not someone other than you. That Self is not someone other than you.

That which makes you draw breath but cannot be drawn by your breath, that is the Self indeed. This Self is not someone other than you.

Kena Upanishad
Translated by Eknath Easwaran (1910-1999)

The first and the most important thing is to know that life is one and immortal. Only the forms, countless in number, are transient and brittle. The life everlasting is independent of any form but manifests itself in all forms. Life then does not die… but the forms are dissolved.

Sri Aurobindo (1872-1950)
Hindu Philosopher, Yogi, Guru and Poet

The Atman—the experiencer—is pure consciousness. It appears to take on the changing colors of the mind. In reality, it is unchangeable.

How to Know God: The Yoga Aphorisms of Patanjali,
translated by Prabhavananda (1893-1976) and Isher-
wood (1904-1986)

Humankind has not woven the web of life. We are but one thread within it.

Whatever we do to the web, we do to ourselves. All things are bound together. All things connect.

Chief Seattle, (1786-1866)
Native American Chief of the Suquamish Tribe

MEDITATION

For when I came into the silent assemblies of God's people I felt a secret power among them which touched my heart, and as I gave way unto it, I found the evil weakening in me and the good raised up.

Robert Barclay (1648-1690)
Scottish Quaker

It is in deep solitude that I find the gentleness with which I can truly love my brothers. The more solitary I am the more affection I have for them. Solitude and silence teach me to love my brothers for what they are, not for what they say.

Father Thomas Merton (1915-1968)
American Catholic Writer, Monk and Mystic

As an archer aims an arrow, the wise aim their restless thoughts, hard to aim, hard to restrain. As a fish hooked an left on the sand thrashes about in agony, the mind being trained in meditation trembles all over, desperate to escape the hand of Mara. Hard it is to train the mind, which goes where it likes and does what it wants. But a trained mind brings health and happiness.

Verses 33-35, The Dhammapada
Collection of Sayings of the Buddha
Translated by Eknath Easwaran (1910-1999)

A talkative soul lacks both the essential virtues and intimacy with God. A deeper interior life, one of gentle peace and of that silence where the Lord dwells, is quite out of the question. A soul that has never tasted the sweetness of inner silence is a restless spirit which disturbs the silence of others.

Saint Mary Faustina Kowalska (1905-1938)
Polish Roman Catholic Nun and Mystic

The purpose of meditation for each of us is that we come to our own center. In many traditions, meditation is spoken of as a pilgrimage—a pilgrimage to your own center, your own heart, and there you learn to remain awake, alive and still. The word 'religion' means a 're-linking', being 'rebound' to your own center. The importance of meditation is to discover from your own experience that there is only one center and that the life task for all of us is to find our source and our meaning by discovering and living out of that one center.

John Main OSB (1926-1982)
Catholic Priest, Monk and Meditation Teacher

Be still and know that I am God.
Be still and know that I am.
Be still and know.
Be still.
Be.

Psalm 46:10 (RSV)

The more you feel peace in meditation, the closer you are to God. He moves nearer and nearer to you the deeper you enter into meditation. The peace of meditation is the language and embracing comfort of God. Therefore, God is present right on the throne of peace within you. Find Him there first and you will find Him in all the noble pursuits of life, in true friends, in the beauty of nature, in good books, in good thoughts, in noble aspirations... When you know God as peace within, then you will realize Him as peace existing in the universal harmony of all things without.

Paramahansa Yogananda (1893-1952)
Founder of the Self-Realization Fellowship

Perhaps one of the greatest rewards of meditation and prayer is the sense of belonging that comes to us.

Bill W. (1895-1971)
Co-Founder of AA

One who has control over the mind is tranquil in heat and cold, in pleasure and pain, and in honor and dishonor; and is ever steadfast with the Supreme Self.

Bhagavad Gita

Many people who come to spiritual practice are frightened by their feelings. They hope meditation will help them to transcend the messiness of the world and leave them invulnerable to difficult feelings. But this is a false transcendence, a denial of life. It is fear masquerading as wisdom.

Jack Kornfield (1945)
Buddhist Monk and Author

You are used to listening to the buzz of the world, but now is the time to develop the inner ear that listens to the inner world. It is time to have a foot in each world, and it can be done.

Saint Bartholomew (1st Century AD)
One of the twelve disciples of Jesus

Yoga is the control [cessation] of thought waves in the mind. Then man abides in his real nature. At other times, when he is not in the state of yoga, man remains identified with the thought-waves in the mind.

How to Know God: The Yoga Aphorisms of Patanjali, translated by Prabhavananda (1893-1976) and Isherwood (1904-1986)

The central benefit of Zen, in the context of ordinary ups and downs of life, is not in preventing the minus and promoting the plus, but in directing people to the fundamental reality that is not under the sway of ups and downs.

Muso Soseki (1275-1351)
Rinzai Zen Buddhist Monk and Poet

The state we call realization is simply be-ing oneself, not knowing anything or be-coming anything.

Ramana Maharishi (1879-1950)
Indian Sage

In zazen, leave your front door and your back door open. Let thoughts come and go. Just don't serve them tea.

Shunryu Suzuki (1904-1971)
Zen Monk

Meditate upon the teacher as the glow of your awareness, When you melt and mingle together, Taste that expanse of nonduality. There remain.

Yeshe Tsogyal (c. 757-817)
Mother of Tibetan Buddhism

A reflective, contented mind is the best possession.

Zoroaster (ca. 1000 BCE)
Iranian prophet and founder of Zoroastrianism

Meditation is evolution in reverse.

Swami Prabhavananda

ABOUT THE CURATOR

Gudjon Bergmann is an author, interfaith minister and musician. He has writ-
ten more than twenty five books—including two novels—on a variety of topics,
ranging from self-improvement to interfaith relations, spirituality and beyond.

For more information visit
www.gudjonbergmann.com

Noteworthy Books by Gudjon Bergmann

Spiritual in My Own Way: Memoir (2019)
Co-Human Harmony (2019)
Experifaith (2017)
Premature Holiness: A Novel (2016)
Baby Steps to Meditation (2014)
Living in the Spirit of Yoga (2010)

Available Albums

Inspired by Rumi (2019)
Eye of the Storm (2020)

Social Media Channels

facebook.com/bergmanngudjon
twitter.com/gudjonbergmann

Made in the USA
Monee, IL
04 August 2021

74964090R00049